Published by:
Nimbus Publishing Limited
P.O. Box 9301, Station A
Halifax, N.S.
B3K 5N5

All book photographs available from:
Master File, Stock Photo Library
415 Yonge Street, Ste. 200
Toronto, Canada
M5B 2E7

Printed in Hong Kong.

Graphic Design: Arthur Carter
Typesetting: A.J. Copyrite Inc.

Cameras: Pentax 6x7
and Contax with Carl Zeiss T. Lens
Film: Fujichrome

Canadian Cataloguing in Publication Data:
Hines, Sherman, 1941-

    Alberta pictorial cookbook

    ISBN 0-921128-15-0 (pbk.)

1. Cookery, Canadian — Prairie style.* 2. Cookery —
Alberta. I. Title.

TX715.H56 1988   641.597123   C88-098533-X

(Right)
Bow Lake with Hector and Balfour Mountains

ALBERTA
A Pictorial
Cookbook

NIMBUS PUBLISHING LIMITED

Introduction

Cattle grazing in the shadow of the foothills reminds us that it was the sun ripened grasses and wide open spaces that lured the first ranchers and cowboys to Alberta. That cowboy legacy lives on in Alberta's celebrations and food traditions. Why else would beef appear at most special occasions, whether roasted in a pit or barbecued in the back yard or roasted to perfection for Sunday dinner?

The flat prairies and rolling parklands attracted homesteaders too. They planted grains where there had been only tough prairie sod and when those waving fields of grain were harvested, they served up splendid spreads of food - succulent roasts, crispy fried chicken, home made bread and pickles, mouthwatering pies and cakes fresh from the oven.

The waving fields of ripening grain are still here and the love of harvest foods remains.

The blueberries, saskatoons and chokecherries growing wild along the banks of Alberta's rivers also remind us of our beginnings. Native Indians dried the delicious berries and stored them in rawhide bags for eating when the snows covered the land. Fur traders who crossed our northern rivers in search of rich fur bearing animals also enjoyed the wild berries, sometimes fresh off the bushes, sometimes in the Indian mixture of dried foods known as pemmican.

When Alberta isn't flat, it's high, and the sight of those ever present Rocky Mountains beckons us toward hiking, skiing and mountain climbing. Outdoor exercise calls for substantial food with robust flavours that match the mountains.

Our history and geography have combined to make us a hearty lot, not so much interested in delicacy as in full flavour and generous amounts.

As well, Albertans bring to the table food traditions and cultures from all over the world which results in exciting and new combinations. So a dinner of British roast beef and Yorkshire pudding might be rounded out with Chinese vegetables and Ukrainian poppy seed cake. It's a flexible feast with new customs and new foods being added all the time.

Alberta is now a thoroughly modern province, keen on its past and its geographical features but also blessed with the newest and biggest of everything. Thus, we have proud cities punctuated by towering glass walls and steel girders, oil pumpers standing next to the ripening wheat, asphalt highways leading over the Northern muskeg. Ours is a land of variety and contrast that has managed a creative blend, a spendid mix.

Photographer Sherman Hines has captured its images; I have tried to capture its truly distinctive tastes. Together, we offer a beautiful and delicious celebration of Alberta.

Bunny Barss, nutritionist, home economist, tour guide and history lover has written several books about Canadian food traditions in a way that captures the essence of Canada and her people.

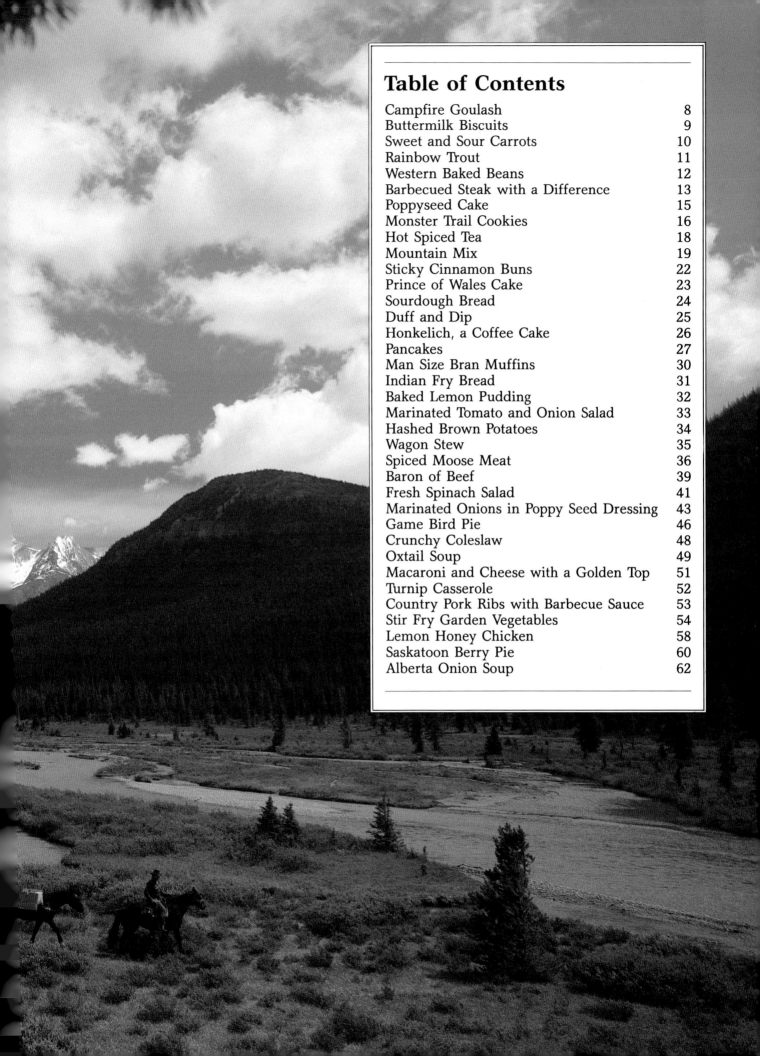

Table of Contents

Imagine a fall day spent hiking in the Rockies, through hillsides covered with golden aspen, over trails hushed by fallen leaves. Then imagine a campfire and this hearty goulash. Imagine it even if you're simply at home in the kitchen.

Campfire Goulash

½ cup/125 ml oil
2 large onions, chopped
4 stalks celery, chopped
2 lbs/1 kg ground beef
2 28 oz/796 ml cans Italian style
    tomatoes
1 5½ oz/156 ml can tomato paste
2 cloves garlic, minced
4 tbsp/60 ml chili powder
2 tbsp/30 ml basil

2 tbsp/30 ml dried parsley
1 tsp/5 ml salt
1½ tsp/7 ml dried mustard
¼ tsp/1 ml black pepper
2 28 oz/796 ml cans red kidney beans
½ cup/125 ml red wine or beer(optional)
¼ lb/222 g pepperoni

Heat oil in a large heavy saucepan and saute onion and celery until slightly soft and yellow. Remove from pan and set aside. In same pan, brown the beef. Return onions and celery to the mixture. Add tomatoes, tomato paste, seasonings, beans and beer or wine. Peel pepperoni and dice. Add it to the main mixture and simmer gently for 15-20 minutes.

Serves 10-12.

Biscuits built the west as surely as railroads and cattle did! They provided a quick treat for visitors, they stretched the family meal, they fed hungry people who had nothing else . . . and they've remained good to this day!

Buttermilk Biscuits

2 cups/500 ml flour
1½ tbsp/25 ml sugar
4 tsp/20 ml baking powder
½ tsp/2 ml salt
½ cup/125 ml melted butter
1 egg, beaten
1 cup/250 ml buttermilk

Place dry ingredients in bowl. Combine melted butter, egg and buttermilk. Add to dry ingredients and beat with electric mixer for about 2 minutes.

Turn mixture out onto well floured board and pat or roll out about ½" (1.5 cm) thick. Cut with biscuit cutter. Bake in a 425°F (210°C) oven for 10-15 minutes or until lightly browned.

Serve with fresh creamy butter and honey. Makes about 24.

Photo: Banff National Park

9

This interesting and flavourful carrot dish can be served as a hot vegetable or cold as a salad. It is best when prepared a day ahead of serving.

Sweet and Sour Carrots

2 lbs/1 kg carrots
1 green pepper
1 medium onion, sliced

Marinade:
1 10 oz/284 ml can tomato soup
¾ cup/175 ml vinegar
⅓ cup/75 ml vegetable oil
¾ cup/175 ml sugar
1 tsp/5 ml prepared mustard
1 tsp/5 ml Worcestershire sauce
1 tsp/5 ml salt
pepper to taste

Peel carrots and cut crosswise in thin rounds. Simmer in salted water for 10 minutes or until just tender-crisp. Drain. Cover with ice water and drain again.

Slice green pepper into thin strips and add with the sliced onion to the carrots.

Mix remaining ingredients in a jar and shake well. Pour over the vegetables. If you wish to serve the vegetables cold, refrigerate at this point for at least 24 hours. If you'd rather have your vegetables hot, place the vegetable mixture into a greased baking dish and bake in a 350°F (180°C) oven for about 30 minutes or until mixture is heated through.

Serves 8-10.

Photo: Calgary

The lower Bow River from Calgary's Fish Creek Park to the irrigation weir at Carseland in southern Alberta is a mecca for fly fishermen. In those waters wait some of the largest and scrappiest brown and rainbow trout found anywhere in the world. The best way to serve such prize fish is as simply and as quickly as possible.

Rainbow Trout

*enough trout to feed the people on hand
enough lemon juice to sprinkle inside
   cavities
enough butter and oil to fry the fish
enough patience to wait for such a
   treat!*

Note: The trout may be rolled in seasoned flour or cornmeal before frying, but most purist fishermen prefer fresh fish fried without too many frills.

Clean trout, remove head, tail and fins. Wash cavity and sprinkle with lemon juice.

Heat butter and oil in frying pan and saute the trout over medium heat, turning once. Allow 10-12 minutes cooking time per inch thickness of fish.

Serve in the outdoors, garnished with early morning sunshine, fresh air and the promise of more good fishing to come!

11

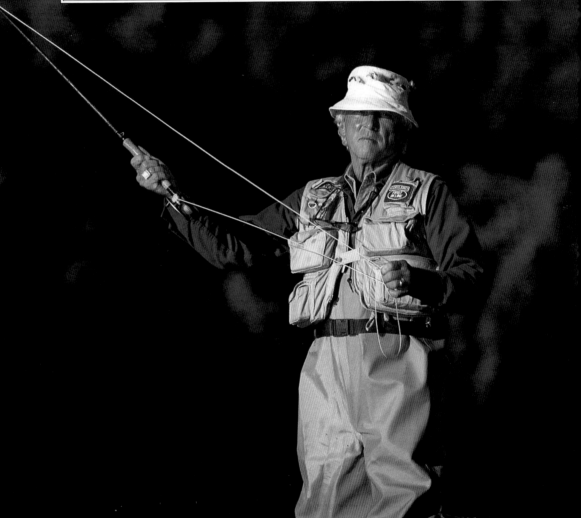

No western barbecue is complete without beef and beans. Beans fed many an early homesteader and rancher and they continue to serve westerners faithfully.

Western Baked Beans

1 28 oz/796 ml can baked beans
1 28 oz/796 ml can red kidney beans
2 14 oz/398 ml cans lima beans
1 19 oz/540 ml can chick peas
¾ cup/200 ml brown sugar
1 tsp/5 ml dry mustard
1 tsp/5 ml salt
½ tsp/2 ml garlic powder
4 tbsp/60 ml ketchup
¾ cup/200 ml vinegar

In a large pot or casserole, combine beans. Mix remaining ingredients together and stir into beans. Cover and bake at 350°F (180°C) for 30 minutes. Remove lid and bake uncovered for another 30 minutes or until hot and bubbly.

Serves 10.

There's more than one way to barbecue a steak. This delicious variation requires a thick sirloin which, when done, is sliced on the diagonal.

Barbecued Steak with a Difference

sirloin steak, 2″ or 5 cm thick
garlic salt
seasoned pepper

Order the steak in advance from a butcher or meat department.

Heat barbecue until coals are very hot. Place steak about 4″ (10 cm) from the coals and barbecue a total of 24-28 minutes for rare, 30-36 minutes for medium and 50-60 for well done. Turn the steak every 10 minutes during this period.

You can use your finger to test for doneness rather than risk losing precious juices by inserting a knife into the meat. If the steak is soft to the touch, it is rare. If it springs back, it is medium and if it is firm, it is well done.

When done, sprinkle both sides with garlic salt and seasoned pepper.

To serve, carve steak across the grain on the diagonal into thin slices – about ¼″ or 1 cm thick. Juices will run out so be sure to catch them for dipping the meat slices.

13

Settlers of Ukrainian origin brought many good tastes to Alberta in the early days . . . like the poppy seed cake below. It is moist and flavourful with a hint of lemon, a crunch of poppy seeds.

Poppyseed Cake

1 cup/250 ml poppy seeds
⅔ cup/150 ml milk
6 eggs
1¼ cups/300 ml oil
1¾ cups/425 ml sugar
2 tsp/10 ml almond flavouring
1 tsp/5 ml vanilla
2 cups/500 ml flour
2 tsp/10 ml baking powder
¼ tsp/1 ml salt

Place poppy seeds in a small bowl, cover with milk and let stand 2-3 hours.

Beat together eggs, oil, sugar, almond flavoring and vanilla. Mix together flour, baking powder and salt. Add to the egg mixture alternately with the milk and poppy seed mixture. Mix well.

Grease and flour a bundt pan or angel food pan. Spoon batter into the pan and bake at 350°F (180°C) for 50-60 minutes or until skewer inserted into the cake comes out clean. After removing from the oven, allow cake to sit in pan for 10 minutes; then turn upside down and carefully remove.

Lemon Glaze: Mix 1 tbsp (15 ml) lemon juice with 3 tbsp (45 ml) icing sugar. While the cake is still warm, pierce the top with a fork in about 15 places. Brush the lemon mixture over the cake and let it soak into the top.

Photos: Colourful poppies heralds summer at Lake Louise. Left: Ethnic dancers at the Calgary Stampede.

In Alberta, the mountains are rugged, the trails are long and the challenges mighty ... which is why you need a few monster cookies in your back pack!

Monster Trail Cookies

1 cup/250 ml margarine
3 cups/750 ml peanut butter
2½ cups/625 ml brown sugar
1 cup/250 ml white sugar
6 eggs
2 tsp/10 ml vanilla
1 tbsp/15 ml corn syrup
4 tsp/20 ml baking soda
1 tsp/5 ml salt
9 cups/2.25L oatmeal
1½ cups/325 ml shelled sunflower seeds

1½ cups/325 ml raisins
1 cup/250 ml chocolate chips

Note: You may use shelled peanuts in place of the sunflower seeds.

In a large bowl, cream together the margarine, peanut butter and sugars. Beat in eggs. Add vanilla, corn syrup, baking soda and salt. Stir in remaining ingredients and mix well.

Drop by heaping tablespoons onto a cookie sheet. Bake in a 350°F (180°C) oven for about 15 minutes or until browned.

Makes about 72 substantial chewy cookies. Enough to get you to the mountain top!

Photo: Crossing Pipestone River, Banff

16

After a day of skiing in the Kananaskis or a skating party on a pond in the Peace River country or a hayride on a snowy evening in Jasper, there's nothing quite as heartwarming as a cup of hot tea. Hot spiced tea to finish a wonderful time in the great outdoors!

Hot Spiced Tea

¾ cup/175 ml instant tea
½ cup/125 ml sugar
1 pkg (3¼ oz)/(92 gm) orange crystals
1 tsp/5 ml cinnamon
¼ tsp/1 ml cloves

Blend ingredients and store in a covered container.

When ready to serve, stir 2-3 tsp (10-15 ml) of the mix with 1 cup (250 ml) boiling water.

Photo: Pipestone Pass Camp

18

Some people climb to the very top of the mountain; others get halfway up; still others barely get off the ground. But everyone takes along some mountain mix!

Mountain Mix

2 cups/500 ml mixed nuts
¼ cup/50 ml shelled sunflower seeds
¼ cup/50 ml shelled pumpkin seeds
½ cup/125 ml chocolate chips

Mix ingredients together, divide into smaller portions and package in plastic bags that can be tucked into knapsacks or pockets, somewhere that's easy to reach.

Note: Buy half salted, half unsalted mixture of nuts. Also, don't use chocolate chips for summer mixtures. Use a coated candy like Smarties instead.

Photo overleaf: Calgary - Saddledome

There's nothing quite like Indian summer in Alberta - when the harvest is safely gathered in, when the hillsides glow with one last burst of color . . . and that's when its time to make sticky cinnamon buns.

Sticky Cinnamon Buns

Sweet roll dough, or bread dough, or frozen bread dough

Sticky Base:
⅓ cup/75 ml butter or margarine
¼ cup/50 ml honey
¼ cup/50 ml brown sugar
1 tbsp/15 ml cinnamon
1 tbsp/15 ml water

To make the bread dough, use a standard sweet roll recipe or plain bread recipe. Or use 2 loaves of frozen bread dough. Whatever method you use to produce the bread dough, have it ready to assemble into buns at this point.

Make the sticky base for the buns by melting the butter or margarine and honey. Stir in sugar, cinnamon and water. Spread to cover the bottom of a 9 x 13" (3.5L) baking pan.

Cinnamon Filling:
¼ cup/50 ml butter or margarine
½ cup/125 ml sugar
3 tbsp/45 ml cinnamon
½ cup/125 ml raisins

Roll bread dough into an oblong of 9 x 18" (23x45 cm). Spread with butter or margarine, sprinkle with sugar, cinnamon and raisins.

Beginning at the wide side, roll up and pinch the edges together. Cut the roll into 1" (2.5 cm) slices and place the slices in the prepared cake pan, leaving a bit of space between each slice.

Cover with a damp tea towel and let rise until double in bulk, 35-40 minutes. If buns are slow to rise, place pan into a warm oven.

Bake at 375°F (190°C) for 25-30 minutes or until buns are nicely browned. Remove from oven and immediately invert the pan so that the buns come out easily.

Will make about 14 buns.

Photo: Aspens shade a roadway in the buffalo compound, Banff

This moist spicy boiled raisin cake was named after the Prince of Wales around 1919 when he purchased the EP Ranch in southern Alberta. It's still served today to tourists who visit the ranch and the teahouse.

Prince of Wales Cake

2 cups/500 ml raisins
2¼ cups/300 ml water
1 cup/250 ml butter or oil
2 cups/500 ml brown sugar
2 eggs
1 tsp/5 ml vanilla
3 cups/750 ml flour
2 tsp/10 ml baking soda
1 tsp/5 ml baking powder
2 tsp/10 ml cinnamon
2 tsp/10 ml nutmeg
1 tsp/5 ml salt

Put raisins and water into a small saucepan and simmer for 4-5 minutes. Cool slightly.

In a large bowl, cream butter or oil, sugar, eggs and vanilla. Mix together dry ingredients and add to the creamed mixture along with the liquid from the raisins. Finally, fold in the raisins.

Pour into a greased and floured 9 x 13" (3.5L) cake pan and bake at 350°F (180°C) for 40-45 minutes or until skewer inserted into the centre of the cake comes out clean.

Frost with Caramel Icing.

Caramel Icing:
⅓ cup/75 ml butter
1½ cups/375 ml icing sugar
⅓ cup/75 ml milk
1 tsp/5 ml vanilla
1-1½/250-375 ml icing sugar

In a heavy saucepan, melt butter. Add icing sugar and stir over low heat for 3 minutes. Add milk and simmer for 3 more minutes, stirring all the while. Remove from heat and cool slightly, about 10 minutes.

Beat in vanilla and enough additional icing sugar to make the frosting stiff enough to spread over the cake.

23

When prospectors headed north from Edmonton to get rich — they hoped — in the North, they often ended up learning more about sourdough than they ever learned about finding gold! Pancakes, bread, buns, biscuits - they were all made from sourdough!

Sourdough Bread

The Sourdough Starter:
1 cup/250 ml skim milk
3 tbsp/45 ml unflavoured yogurt
1 cup/250 ml flour

Warm milk, add yogurt and let stand covered in a warm place for one day. Add flour and let stand, covered, in a warm place for another 2-5 days. If mixture separates, stir carefully.

This is the starter. Whenever you use a portion, replace with 1 cup (250 ml) flour and 1 cup (250 ml) warm milk. Let stand 24 hours after each addition before using again. If you're not going to be using the starter for several days, slow down the action by placing in the refrigerator or freezer.

The Sourdough Bread:
1 tbsp/15 ml dry yeast
1½ cups/375 ml lukewarm water
1 cup/250 ml sourdough starter
2 tbsp/30 ml sugar
2 tsp/10 ml salt
4 cups/1 L flour
½ tsp/2 ml baking soda
½ cup/125 ml flour

In a large bowl, dissolve yeast in warm water. Stir in sourdough starter, sugar and salt. Stir in flour, one cup at a time, mixing well. Dough will be sticky. Cover with a cloth and leave in a warm place until doubled in size - about 1½ hours.

Mix baking soda and remaining flour together. Sprinkle over dough and mix in. Turn out onto lightly floured board and knead until satiny and soft. Divide into four pieces and shape into loaves.

Place on a greased cookie sheet. Make 2 or 3 slashes about ¼" (1 cm) deep in top of each loaf. Let stand in a warm place until doubled - about 40 minutes. Bake at 375°F (190°C) for 30 minutes or until lightly browned.

Home on the range, years ago, the chuckwagon cook would occasionally treat the cowboys to a dessert called Duff and Dip. It was a steamed pudding served with a variety of sauces . . . and that's what it remains today!

Duff and Dip

1 cup/250 ml raisins
1 cup/250 ml currants
1 cup/250 ml grated carrots
1 cup/250 ml grated potatoes
1 cup/250 ml soft butter
1¼ cups/300 ml flour
¾ cup/200 ml sugar
1 tsp/5 ml baking soda
1 tsp/5 ml salt
1 tsp/5 ml nutmeg
½ tsp/2 ml cinnamon

Note: You may use 1 cup (250 ml) grated suet in place of the butter.

Wash raisins and currants. Set aside.

Combine carrots, potatoes and butter. Mix dry ingredients together, stir in raisins and currants. Add to the first mixture. Spoon into a greased 1½ qt. (1.5L) mold - it should be about ⅔ full.

Cover with two layers of foil and tie down with a string. Place a metal stand or jar ring on the bottom of a kettle or Dutch oven. Pour several inches of water into the kettle or oven, and place the filled mold on the stand so the water covers ⅓ to ½ of the mold. Cover the kettle and steam for about 3 hours. The pudding will be firm and a toothpick or skewer when inserted will come out clean.

When done, unmold, wrap and store in the refrigerator for 1-2 weeks to season, or freeze for longer storage. To reheat, steam for an hour or place foil wrapped pudding in a 300°F (150°C) oven for an hour.

Serve with Brandy or Rum Sauce.

Brandy or Rum Sauce:
¾ cup/175 ml brown sugar
½ cup/125 ml corn syrup
¼ cup/50 ml butter
dash of salt
1 tbsp/15 ml cornstarch
1 cup/250 ml water
1 tbsp/15 ml rum or brandy

In a heavy saucepan, simmer sugar, corn syrup, butter and salt for about 4 minutes, stirring frequently. Mix cornstarch with about half the water and stir in.

Add remaining water and simmer for 2-3 minutes. Remove from heat and add flavoring.

Old meets new in the approximately 170 Hutterite colonies in Alberta. Agriculture is carried out with the very newest machinery but residents still wear traditional clothing, tasks are still divided along traditional lines, cooking is still done according to the principle of ''Waste not, want not''.

Honkelich, a Coffee Cake

*Basic sweet dough, biscuit dough or
  frozen bread dough*
½ cup/125 ml whipping cream
1 egg yolk
⅓ cup/75 ml soft butter
½ cup/125 ml flour

½ cup/125 ml brown sugar
½ tsp/2 ml cinnamon

To make this quick treat, Hutterite women just use a piece of their regular bread dough. However, if you're not a regular bread maker, use 1 loaf frozen dough or 1 recipe of basic biscuit dough.

Grease a 9 x 13'' (22x33 cm) pan. Spread the dough over bottom of pan. Brush with cream. Mix egg yolk, butter, flour and sugar. Spread this crumbly mixture over the cream. Dust with cinnamon.

Let rise until double and then bake at 350°F (180°C) for 20-30 minutes until lightly browned.

Serve hot from the oven.

A pancake by any other name is a flapjack, a griddle cake, a hotcake, a quick way to make a breakfast or a meal. Bachelors relied on them in the early days - until they could find themselves a wife — and modern festivities like the Calgary Stampede continue to rely on this faithful standby.

Pancakes

2 eggs
2 cups/500 ml milk
2 tbsp/30 ml sugar
2 tbsp/30 ml oil
2 cups/500 ml flour
1 tbsp/15 ml baking powder
½ tsp/2 ml salt

Note: Instead of 2 cups (500 ml) white flour, you could use a mixture of white flour, whole wheat flour and cornmeal.

Beat eggs, milk, sugar and oil until well blended. Mix dry ingredients together, add to the egg mixture and beat well.

Grease a frying pan or griddle and drop spoonsful of batter onto hot surface. When pancakes bubble, turn and cook the other side.

Serve with maple syrup, mock maple syrup or homemade jams. Serves 2-4.

Photo overleaf: The Claresholm grain elevators stand like sentinels

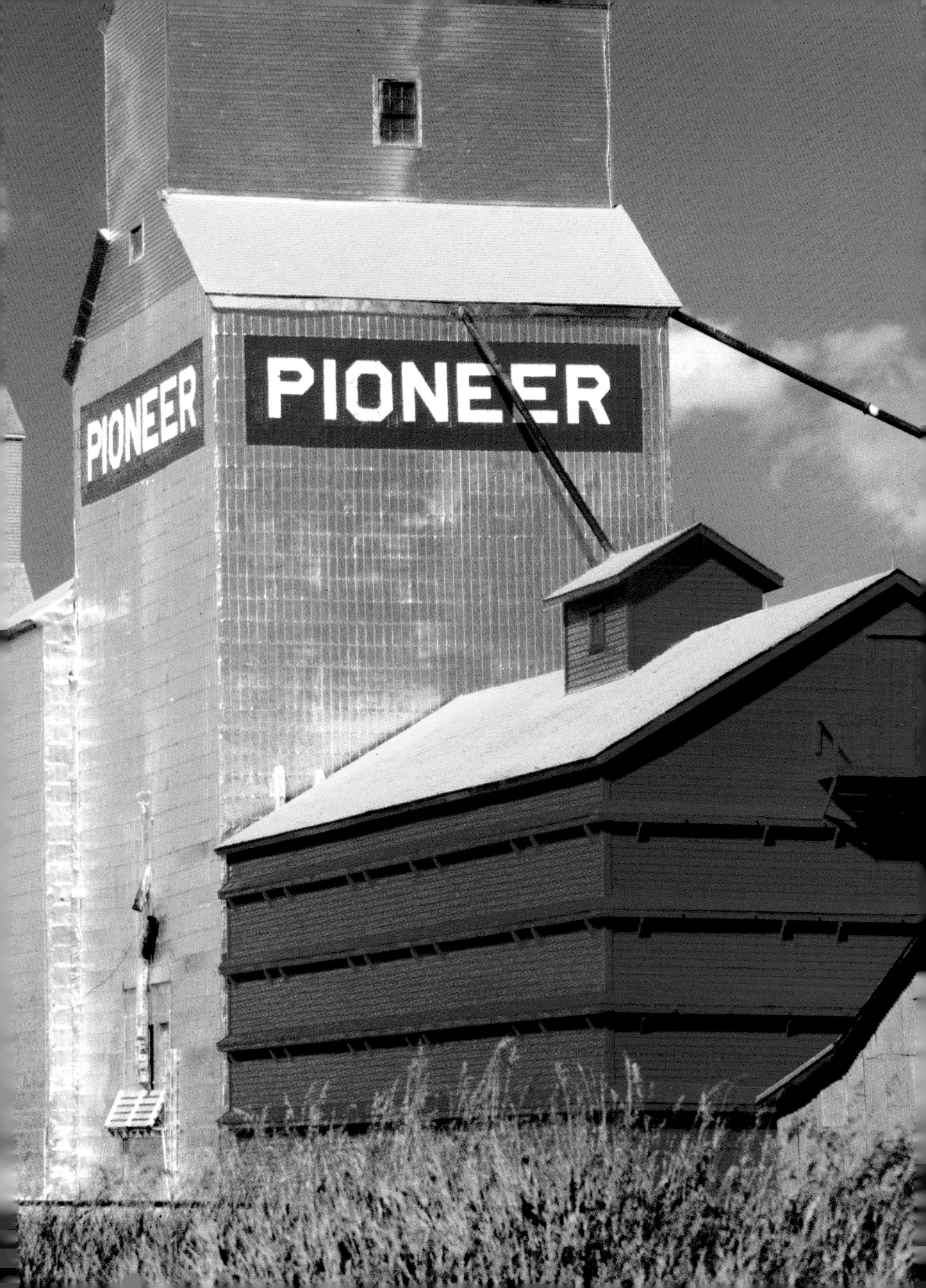
PIONEER
PIONEER

Talk to an Albertan and you'll find someone who remembers the threshing crews that came every fall to help with the harvest, and how the women of the family had to come up with three huge meals a day ... not to mention hearty snacks like Bran Muffins.

Man Size Bran Muffins

5 tsp/25 ml baking soda
2 cups/500 ml boiling water
1 cup/250 ml butter or margarine
2 cups/500 ml sugar
4 eggs
4 cups/1L buttermilk
1 tbsp/15 ml salt
5 cups/1.25L flour
2 cups/500 ml 40% bran cereal

4 cups/1L all bran cereal
2 cups/500 ml chopped dates

Note: This recipe can be prepared ahead and stored in the refrigerator for up to two weeks. Just use as much as you need for each occasion.

Add baking soda to boiling water and let cool.

Cream butter or margarine with sugar, add eggs and beat well.

Stir in buttermilk, salt and flour.

Mix cereals with the cooled water and baking soda mixture. Add to the flour mixture. Stir in dates. Store in covered container in the refrigerator.

When baking, fill greased muffin tins ⅔ full of batter and bake at 400°F (200°C) for 20-25 minutes.

Photo: Pincher Creek

When the buffalo disappeared and with it the Indian way of life, Indians had to find new food traditions. One that they learned from the fur traders was bannock or fry bread. Today, it is considered an Indian specialty, featured at such celebrations as the Calgary Stampede and the opening of Head Smashed In Buffalo Jump in southern Alberta.

Indian Fry Bread

3 cups/750 ml flour
3 tbsp/45 ml baking powder
1 tsp/5 ml salt
2 tbsp/30 ml melted lard
1½ cups/375 ml water

Combine dry ingredients. Make a depression in centre and pour in melted lard and water. Mix into a soft dough and gently knead a few times.

To fry: Shape the dough into a flat piece. Cut into rectangles. Heat about ½″ (1.5 cm) of hot fat in a frying pan. Drop a few pieces of dough into the hot fat. When browned on one side, turn over and brown other side. Drain on paper towels.

Also, you could use a deep fat fryer set at 375°F (190°C). Fry each piece of dough until brown on both sides.

Serve hot with strawberry jam.

Photo: An Indian woman at the Calgary Stampede

Like splendid sunsets that make a good day even better, so does a tangy lemon dessert finish off an already wonderful meal.

Baked Lemon Pudding

¾ cup/200 ml sugar
4 tbsp/60 ml flour
¼ tsp/1 ml salt
2 tbsp/30 ml margarine, melted
1 tsp/5 ml grated lemon rind
⅓ cup/75 ml lemon juice
2 egg yolks
1¼ cups/300 ml milk
2 egg whites

In large bowl, combine sugar, flour, salt, melted margarine, lemon rind, lemon juice and egg yolks. Mix together. Add milk and stir.

Beat egg whites until stiff and fold into batter.

Pour into a buttered 8″ (1L) casserole dish. Set casserole dish into a pan of water and bake at 350°F (180°C) for 45-50 minutes, or until cake top springs back when touched lightly with finger.

Serve warm or cold. Makes 4 servings.

Photo: The Hoodoos, near Drumheller

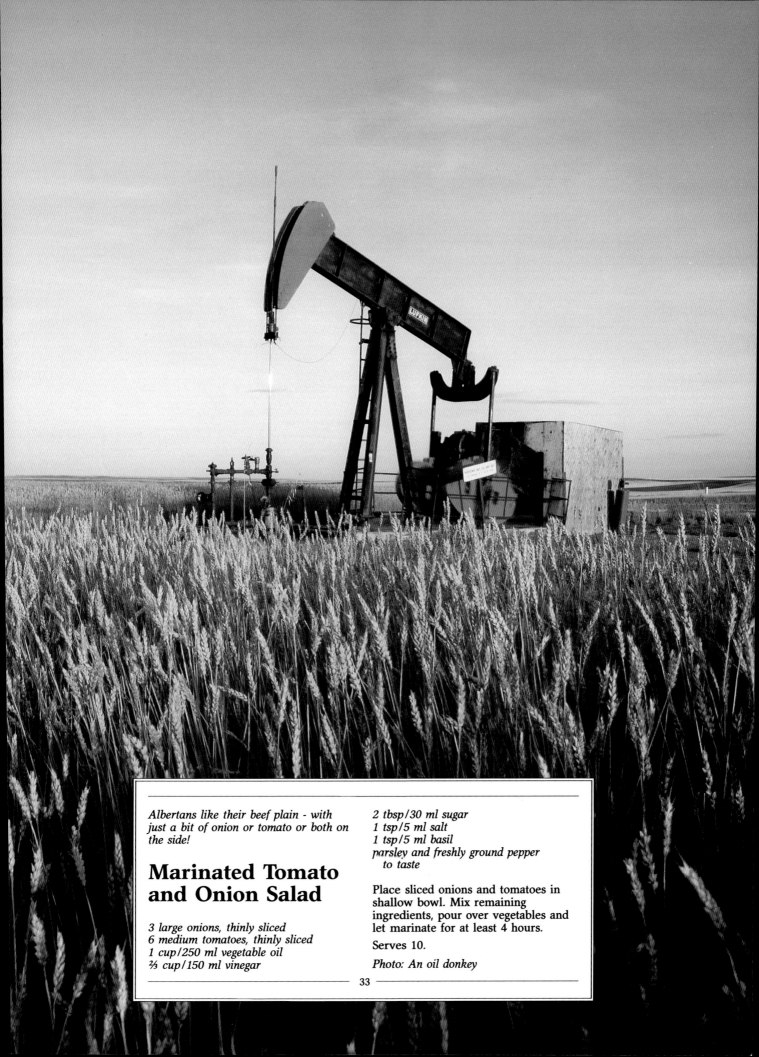

Albertans like their beef plain - with just a bit of onion or tomato or both on the side!

Marinated Tomato and Onion Salad

3 large onions, thinly sliced
6 medium tomatoes, thinly sliced
1 cup/250 ml vegetable oil
⅔ cup/150 ml vinegar

2 tbsp/30 ml sugar
1 tsp/5 ml salt
1 tsp/5 ml basil
parsley and freshly ground pepper to taste

Place sliced onions and tomatoes in shallow bowl. Mix remaining ingredients, pour over vegetables and let marinate for at least 4 hours.

Serves 10.

Photo: An oil donkey

Hashed brown potatoes are the dressed up version of fried potatoes that formed the backbone of so many meals in earlier days in Alberta. Then, it was thought that a day without spuds was a day without real food!

Hashed Brown Potatoes

*4 medium potatoes
salt and freshly ground pepper
  to taste
2 tbsp/30 ml butter
2 tbsp/30 ml oil*

Boil potatoes in their jackets for about 10 minutes or until they are just slightly firm. Drain and peel. Grate with a medium coarse grater. Sprinkle with salt and pepper.

Heat butter and oil in a heavy frying pan or grill. Fry the potatoes on one side until crispy golden brown, then turn with a spatula and fry the other side until equally brown.

Serves 4.

*Stew served the west well in the early
days - days when the chuckwagon cook
had to provide hearty meals from one
large pot, days when homesteaders had
to stretch every resource ... which is
why westerners still like the taste of a
hearty homemade stew.*

Wagon Stew

2 lbs/1 kg stewing meat
2 tbsp/30 ml beef fat or lard
4 tbsp/60 ml flour
2 medium onions, sliced
2 cups/500 ml water
1 cup/250 ml canned tomatoes
1 tsp/5 ml chili powder
salt and pepper to taste
vegetables and parsley

Cut meat into 2″ (5 cm) cubes. Melt
the beef fat or lard in a heavy pan or
Dutch oven with a tightly fitting lid.
If using beef fat, discard the bits of
residue. Add the meat and brown.
Sprinkle flour over meat and toss
lightly. Add onions, water, tomatoes,
chili powder, salt and pepper. Cover
and bake at 300°F (150°C) or simmer
on top of the stove for approximately
3 hours or until tender. Cooking time
depends on the cut of the meat.

Add vegetables such as turnips,
carrots, parsnips and potatoes about
30 minutes before stew is to be
served. Add peas about 5 minutes
before serving. Sprinkle chopped
parsley on top when serving.

Serves 4-6.

*Photo: Abandoned farm wagon near
Blackie*

This is a lovely blend of old and new. Moosemeat fed many an early homesteader but in this recipe, it's updated to belong on the most modern table!

Spiced Moose Meat

16 lbs/8 kg moosemeat
1 cup/250 ml coarse pickling salt
1 cup/250 ml brown sugar
1 tbsp/15 ml saltpetre
1 tbsp/15 ml each cinnamon, allspice, cloves, mace, nutmeg
1 tbsp/15 ml coarse black pepper

Note: The best cut for this treatment is half of the round. Saltpetre is available at drugstores.

With kitchen cord, tie meat into a solid round piece. Rub salt over outside and let stand overnight. In the morning, mix sugar, saltpetre and spices together and rub into the meat. Place meat in a crock or in two layers of heavy plastic bags - in case one tears. Place in the back of the refrigerator or in some other cool place for 2-3 weeks to allow spices to penetrate. Turn every day.

At end of curing period, drain the meat, wrap in foil and bake in a roasting pan in a 275°F (135°C) oven for 6 hours.

Delicious for Christmas parties when thinly sliced and served with bread and mustard sauce.

Ever since the early ranchers discovered the wide open ranges in southern Alberta, beef has been king. There are fences now and every other kind of domesticated meat available - including caribou and antelope farms - but beef still reigns . . . which means that the ability to turn out a good roast of beef is very important in this province!

Baron of Beef

If you're planning a party for 40 or more, you can order a whole hip of beef. Sear it on the outside and then barbecue or roast slowly for approximately 20 minutes per pound, 50 minutes per kg.

However, if you're not having the whole neighborhood over, you may want to use just the top part of the hip roast - otherwise known as the baron. Ask your butcher to make it into a long boneless easy-to-carve roast, resembling a rolled prime rib. In fact, you could use a rolled prime rib. Both cuts produce a very tasty tender roast. Count on 1 lb (500 g) serving 2 people.

Place on a rack in a roasting pan. If oven space is a problem, stand roast on end. Roast, uncovered, at 300°F (150°C) until meat thermometer reads 140°F (60°C) for rare meat, 160°F (75°C) for medium done, 170°F (90°C) for well done. It is usually safest to roast to medium and then serve outside cuts to those who want their meat well or medium well done, reserving inside cuts for those who like it rare.

As you carve and serve meat, spoon on juices left in pan.

Another Beef Roasting Method: Necessity being the mother of invention, busy homemakers in the west have discovered how to have a roast ready for the gang after a day of skiing or backpacking or working in the field. Put a large roast in a 400°F (200°C) oven for 1 hour in the morning, then turn the oven down to the desired final temperature at which you want the meat. That is, if you want the roast to be medium rare or 140°F (60°C), you'd turn the oven to that temperature and leave it until you're home. If it's not quite roasted as much as you want, you can always turn up the oven at the end of the time.

Photo: Wheat remains Alberta's chief agricultural crop, Inset: Stampede Parade, Calgary

Alberta beef needs a full bodied salad - something like this spinach salad which could be served before or with the main course.

Fresh Spinach Salad

8-10 cups/2-2.5 L fresh spinach
2 green onions
2 tbsp/30 ml red wine vinegar
6 tbsp/90 ml salad oil
2 tsp/10 ml honey
1 tsp/5 ml dry mustard
½ tsp/2 ml salt
¼ tsp/1 ml pepper
6 slices bacon
2 eggs, hardcooked

Wash and dry spinach. Tear into bite sized pieces. Chop green onions, stems and all, and add to the spinach. Refrigerate in a plastic bag until ready to serve.

In a jar with tight fitting lid, shake together vinegar, salad oil, honey, mustard, salt and pepper. Fry bacon until crisp and crumble into small pieces. Chop eggs.

To put salad together, put greens into a large bowl, toss with dressing, add bacon and garnish with egg.

Serves 6-8.

41

Beef-on-a-bun is often served at large gatherings in Alberta, and when it's dressed up with onions and sour cream, it's no wonder there are so many large gatherings!

Marinated Onions in Poppy Seed Dressing

1 large Spanish onion
⅓ cup/75 ml oil
⅔ cup/150 ml vinegar
1 cup/250 ml water
1 tsp/5 ml sugar
1 tsp/5 ml salt
1 cup/250 ml sour cream
1 tbsp/15 ml poppy seeds

Slice the onion in thin slices. Combine oil, vinegar, water, sugar and salt and pour over the onions. Let marinate 2-3 hours. Drain thoroughly.

Pour sour cream over onions, mix briefly and then sprinkle with poppy seeds.

Serve with beef. Serves 8-10.

Photos: Calgary

43

Fall colours are glorious in Alberta - the burning yellow aspens in the mountains, the brilliant red wild rose berries, the dull gold harvest fields. It's a season that's particularly appreciated by hunters.

Game Bird Pie

4-5 cups/1-1.25 L cooked game bird
6 tbsp/90 ml butter or margarine
1 large onion, chopped
2 cups/500 ml sliced mushrooms
2 tbsp/30 ml chopped pimiento
6 tbsp/90 ml flour
2 cups/500 ml reserved stock
1½ cups/375 ml light cream
½ cup/125 ml white wine
2 tsp/10 ml Worcestershire sauce
1 tsp/5 ml salt
¾ tsp/3 ml sage
½ tsp/2 ml thyme
¼ tsp/1 ml pepper
pastry for top crust of 9" (23 cm) pie

Note: Two pheasants will yield enough meat for this pie; most other game birds - grouse, partridge, prairie chicken - will yield slightly less. To prepare the meat, place plucked, cleaned, cut up birds in a heavy sauce pan or Dutch oven. Fill pot half full of water. Add 1 tsp (5 ml) celery seed and 1 tbsp (15 ml) dried parsley. Simmer gently for 2-2 ½ hours or until meat comes away from bones easily. Remove meat in strips from bones and set aside. Save the stock.

Now to make the pie, place the cooked meat into a 3 qt (3L) deep casserole dish. Melt butter in a sauce pan and saute onion until tender. Add mushrooms and pimiento and saute lightly. Stir in flour, then slowly add the reserved stock and light cream. Simmer and stir until thickened. Add wine and seasonings and stir to combine well.

Pour sauce over game in dish. Roll out pastry and place over top. Make 3-4 slits in pastry for steam to escape. Bake at 350°F (180°C) for 1 hour or until lightly browned and bubbling inside. Can be made ahead and frozen.

Serves 6-8.

Photo: Rose Hip, Right: Partridge

German settlers introduced coleslaw to the Canadian prairies - where it took very well and has been enjoyed ever since!

Crunchy Coleslaw

½ head cabbage
2 tbsp/30 ml chopped green onions
2 tbsp/30 ml vinegar
½ cup/125 ml vegetable oil
3 tbsp/45 ml sugar
1 tsp/5 ml salt
¼ tsp/1 ml pepper
1 cup/250 ml fried Oriental noodles
2 tbsp/30 ml slivered almonds
2 tsp/10 ml sesame seeds

Note: Fried Oriental noodles are available in the soup section of the supermarket. Use just the noodles in the package, not the spices which are also enclosed.

Shred cabbage to make about 4 cups (1L). Add onions.

In a jar, shake together vinegar, vegetable oil, sugar, salt and pepper. Toss with the cabbage and refrigerate for several hours.

Just before serving, toss in noodles, almonds and sesame seeds.

Serves 4-5.

Photo: Spring thaw on the Bow River

Oxtail soup (which is really just a delicious beef based soup) came to the west with the early ranchers and stayed here because it was so good!

Oxtail Soup

1½ lbs/700 g oxtails
2 tbsp/30 ml flour
10 cups/2.5L water
2 medium onions, sliced
1 bay leaf
½ cup/125 ml barley
2 cups/500 ml canned tomatoes
3 carrots, diced
1 tbsp/15 ml Worcestershire sauce
1½ tsp/7 ml salt
freshly ground pepper to taste

Trim the fat from the oxtails and place them in a heavy Dutch oven. When the fat has been rendered, pour it off and brown the oxtails. After they are well browned, toss flour over them and brown slightly. Add the water, onions and bay leaf. Cover and simmer for 2 hours or bake in a 300°F (150°C) oven for the same length of time.

Rinse barley in warm water. Add to the soup along with the remaining ingredients. Simmer or bake for another hour. Add more water if the soup is too thick.

Serves 6-8.

Photo: A boathouse marks the edge of frozen Maligne Lake

*Alberta's grain fields are its oceans -
wave upon wave of green and gold
moving with the winds. One of the wheat
varieties - Durum - makes pasta products
the equal of anything in the world.*

Macaroni and Cheese With a Golden Top

1 cup/250 ml uncooked macaroni
1 egg, slightly beaten
1 cup/250 ml milk
¼ tsp/1 ml dry mustard
¼ tsp/1 ml Worcestershire sauce
1 cup/250 ml grated Cheddar cheese

Cook macaroni in boiling salted water
until just tender. Drain. Add
remaining ingredients. Turn into a
buttered casserole dish and spread
with topping, recipe below. Bake at
400°F (200°C) for 15 minutes or until
top is crunchy and golden.

Macaroni Topping:
⅓ cup/75 ml melted butter
20 soda crackers, crushed
¾ cup/200 ml grated Cheddar cheese

Mix together and spread over
macaroni.

Serves 2-3.

Albertans say "turnip" and other parts of the country say "rutabaga" but they're one and the same thing . . . a hearty tasty root vegetable. In this recipe, the turnips are softened by the carrots, a nice combination.

Turnip Casserole

2 medium turnips
2 large carrots
3 tbsp/45 ml butter
1 tsp/5 ml salt
¼ tsp/1 ml pepper
2 eggs, beaten
1½ cups/375 ml bread crumbs
1½ tbsp/25 ml melted butter

Cook turnips and carrots until tender. Drain well. Mash and drain again. Add butter, salt, pepper and beaten eggs. Spoon into a buttered casserole dish.

Toss bread crumbs with melted butter and sprinkle over casserole. Bake at 350°F (180°C) for 30-45 minutes or until casserole puffs.

You could make this in advance and refrigerate until about an hour before you plan to serve the meal. Then bake for about an hour.

Photo: Near Red Deer

52

A hearty meal - a good match for a day of skiing, a week of harvesting, a time of visiting.

Country Pork Ribs with Barbecue Sauce

2 lbs/1 kg spare ribs
1 cup/250 ml vinegar
2 tbsp/30 ml sugar
2 tbsp/30 ml Worcestershire sauce
½ cup/125 ml ketchup
1 tsp/5 ml dry mustard
1 tsp/5 ml salt
dash of freshly ground pepper
1 clove garlic, minced

Place spare ribs on a rack in a large roasting pan and bake, uncovered, in 450°F (230°C) oven for 15 minutes.

Put remaining ingredients into a sauce pan, cover and simmer for 15 minutes.

Drain fat from roasting pan, brush spare ribs on both sides with barbecue sauce. Bake for 1 hour covered and ½ hour uncovered. Baste occasionally with remaining sauce.

Serves 4-5.

Gardens are alive and well in Alberta - small backyard gardens or market gardens or the acres of commercial gardens that characterize parts of southern Alberta. Chinese cooking is alive and well too, and this recipe combines the two.

Stir Fry Garden Vegetables

3 tbsp/45 ml vegetable oil
2 cloves garlic, minced
¼ cup/50 ml chopped onion
1 tsp/5 ml grated ginger
1½ cups/325 ml broccoli
1 cup/250 ml cauliflower
3 carrots
3 stalks celery
1 red pepper
¼ cup/50 ml almonds, toasted
½ cup/125 ml chicken stock
2 tsp/10 ml cornstarch
2 tbsp/30 ml soy sauce

Note: A wok works best for a stir fry recipe, of course, but if you don't have one, use a large heavy frying pan. Also, you can use many other vegetables besides the ones listed above - green beans, bean sprouts, pea pods, tomatoes, mushrooms and zucchini to name just a few.

Prepare everything before beginning the stir fry. Keep garlic, onions and ginger together. Cut broccoli and cauliflower into bite sized pieces and keep together. Slice carrots, celery and red pepper into thin diagonal slices and keep together. Toast the almonds.

If you don't have chicken stock on hand, use a chicken bouillon cube dissolved in ½ cup (125 ml) hot water. Mix with cornstarch and soy sauce.

Now, heat the oil in the wok or frying pan. Stir in garlic, onion and ginger. Stir for a minute. Add broccoli and cauliflower, stir 1½ minutes. Add carrots, celery and pepper and stir another 1½ minutes. Add sauce, cover and cook for 2 minutes, stirring occasionally, or until vegetables are tender crisp.

Top with toasted almonds just before serving. Serves 4.

Photo: Calgary
Overleaf: Waterton National Park

A dressed-up version of chicken - good for a Sunday dinner with good friends. A glass of wine, a loaf of bread . . . and a good time!

Lemon Honey Chicken

1 frying chicken, cut up, or thighs
  and breasts
¾ cup/200 ml flour
½ tsp/2 ml salt
¼ tsp/1 ml each pepper and paprika
4 tbsp/60 ml butter

Prepare chicken pieces. Combine flour, salt, pepper and paprika. Melt butter in bottom of a large flat roaster or baking dish. Roll chicken pieces in the melted butter and then in the flour mixture. Place chicken in a single layer in the baking dish, skin side up, and bake uncovered in 400°F (200°C) oven for 30 minutes.

Drizzle Lemon Honey Sauce over top and continue baking at the same temperature for another 30 minutes.

Lemon Honey Sauce:
½ cup/125 ml lemon juice
¼ cup/50 ml oil
2 tbsp/30 ml chopped onion
1 tbsp/15 ml honey
1 tsp/5 ml Dijon mustard
½ tsp/2 ml salt
¼ tsp/1 ml pepper

Mix ingredients together, drizzle over chicken and bake as above.

Photo: Edmonton

Saskatoons are a treat in the springtime when their blossoms dress up hillsides and ditches but it's in summer that they really come into their own - when the berries are ripe and literally hang off the branches. Then they almost ask to be made into that old favourite - Saskatoon Pie!

Saskatoon Berry Pie

pastry for a 2 crust 9'' (23 cm) pie
4 cups/1 L saskatoons
¼ cup/50 ml water
2 tbsp/30 ml lemon juice
1 cup/250 ml sugar
3 tbsp/45 ml flour
¼ tsp/1 ml salt
1 tsp/5 ml grated lemon rind

Prepare pastry and cover bottom of pie plate.

Simmer saskatoons and water in a covered saucepan for 5 minutes. Add lemon juice, sugar, flour, salt and lemon rind. Pour into uncooked pastry shell. Top with another layer of pastry. Press edges together with a fork and make several slits in top for the steam to escape.

Bake at 400°F (200°C) for 40-45 minutes or until lightly browned and fruit is tender. Serve with thick cream or ice cream.

Photo: Young male elk (or wapati) in Jasper

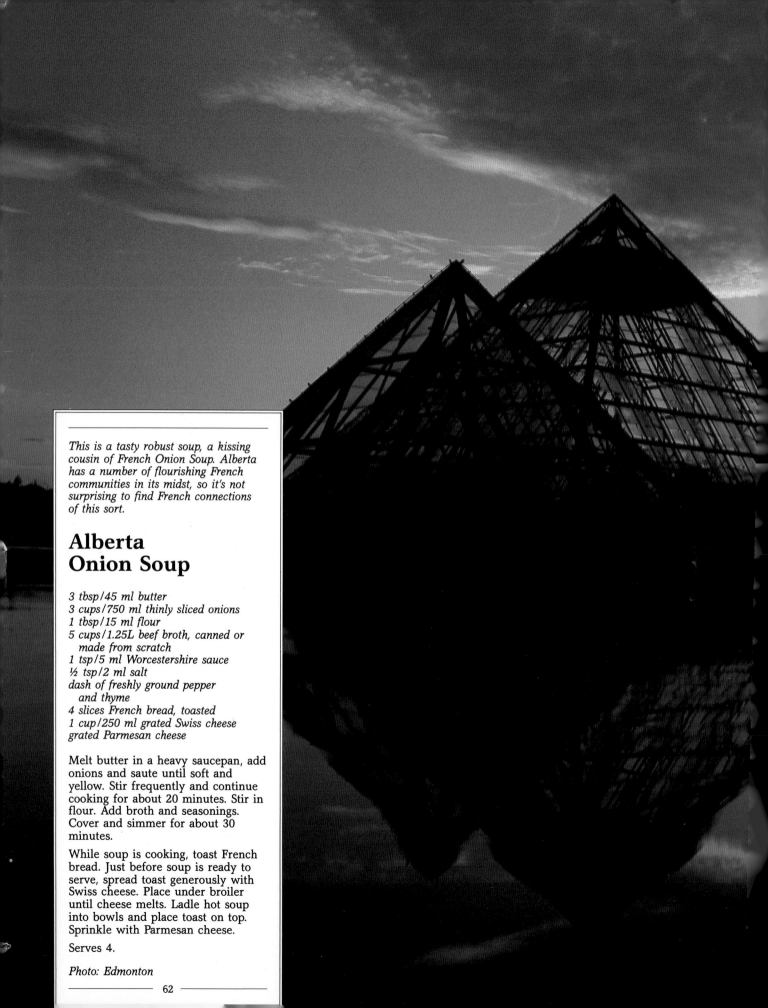

This is a tasty robust soup, a kissing cousin of French Onion Soup. Alberta has a number of flourishing French communities in its midst, so it's not surprising to find French connections of this sort.

Alberta Onion Soup

3 tbsp/45 ml butter
3 cups/750 ml thinly sliced onions
1 tbsp/15 ml flour
5 cups/1.25L beef broth, canned or made from scratch
1 tsp/5 ml Worcestershire sauce
½ tsp/2 ml salt
dash of freshly ground pepper and thyme
4 slices French bread, toasted
1 cup/250 ml grated Swiss cheese
grated Parmesan cheese

Melt butter in a heavy saucepan, add onions and saute until soft and yellow. Stir frequently and continue cooking for about 20 minutes. Stir in flour. Add broth and seasonings. Cover and simmer for about 30 minutes.

While soup is cooking, toast French bread. Just before soup is ready to serve, spread toast generously with Swiss cheese. Place under broiler until cheese melts. Ladle hot soup into bowls and place toast on top. Sprinkle with Parmesan cheese.

Serves 4.

Photo: Edmonton